What are we learning?

What will we learn this week?

New Words

We will learn lots of **verbs**, SOME of the verbs we will learn are on the next page, but we will learn many more. We will learn **3 parts of the verb**. Not just eat, but **eat, ate and eaten**.

Grammar

We will learn about the **PRESENT PERFECT** tense. Sentences such as **I have already eaten lunch** and **I haven't eaten lunch yet**.

Reading

We will read two texts. **One fiction** and **one non-fiction**. Both about newspapers. We will learn many new words and answer **comprehension questions**. We will learn how to write **extended answers**. (NOT just one or two sentences!)

Writing

We will learn how to **write a newspaper**. We will learn about the different sections of a newspaper and then have a go at creating our own paper!

And Fun!

We will also play lots of games and have lots of fun!

Learn Some Words

All verbs have three different forms, let's learn all three!

talk	laugh	run	buy
talked	laughed	ran	bought
talked	laughed	run	bought

eat	go	write	read
ate	went	wrote	read
eaten	gone	written	read

Grammar

He has already walked the dog He hasn't walked the dog yet

He hasn't eaten his bun yet,
(see it's still in his hand)

He's already eaten his bun
(it's in his belly now!)

Make sentences What have you done today **I've........**

1. walked the dog
2. washed her hands
3. fed the dog
4. taken a shower
5. eaten a bun
6. gone to school
7. written homework
8. read a book

Ask and answer questions with your classmates

Have you walked the dog yet? Yes, I have No, I haven't

Practice

Complete these questions, (however you like) and ask your classmates.

Have you eaten dinner yet?	*Yes, I have*
Have you ____________ yet?	________
Have you ____________ yet?	________
Have you ____________ yet?	________
____________________yet?	________
____________________yet?	________
____________________yet?	________
_______________________?	________
_______________________?	________
_______________________?	________
_______________________?	________
_______________________?	________
_______________________?	________
_______________________?	________
_______________________?	________
_______________________?	________
_______________________?	________
_______________________?	________
_______________________?	________

More Words

Let's learn some more words, what verbs do you know, and what is the third form of them – write them down here:

Have Some Fun

Play memory – your teacher is going to put the cards face down, let's see if you can remember where you are! Write the words you got here:

____

____

A Newspaper Story

The New York Mirror was a newspaper that published in New York. Below is a story about this newspaper.

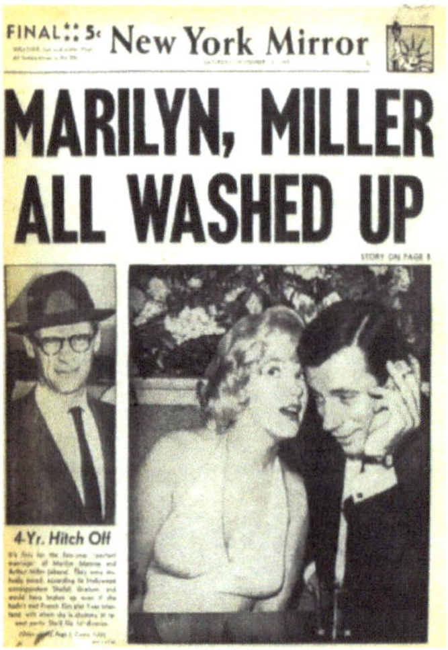
FINAL 5¢ New York Mirror

MARILYN, MILLER ALL WASHED UP

4-Yr. Hitch Off

Some Words

Before we read the story let's check some difficult words. Please write IN ENGLISH the meaning of these words:

classiest ______________________________

dame ______________________________

jealous ______________________________

plotted ______________________________

reporter ______________________________

glorious ______________________________

poison ______________________________

honeymoon ______________________________

Snow White in New York

Once upon a time in New York there was a poor little rich girl called Snow White. Her mother was dead and for a while she lived happily with her father. But one day he married again...

All the papers said Snow White's stepmother was the classiest dame in New York. But no one knew she was Queen of the Underworld. She liked to see herself in the *New York Mirror.* But one day she read something that made her very jealous – 'Snow White the Belle of New York City' – and she plotted to get rid of her stepdaughter.

'Take her down and shoot her,' she said to one of her bodyguards.

The man took Snow White deep into the dark streets, but he could not do it. He left her there, lost and alone.

Snow White wandered the streets all night, tired and hungry. In the early morning she heard music coming from an open door. She went inside.

The seven jazz men were sorry for her, 'Stay here if you like,' they said, 'but you will have to work.'

'What can I do?' she asked.

'Can you sing?' asked one of them.

The very first night Snow White sang there was a reporter in the club. He knew at once that she would be a star.

Next day Snow White was on the front page of the *New York Mirror.* The stepmother was mad with rage. 'This time I shall get rid of her myself,' she said.

And so she decided to hold a grand party in honor of Snow White's success... but...secretly she dropped a poisoned cherry in a cocktail and handed it to Snow White with a smile.

All New York was shocked by the death of the beautiful Snow White.

Crowds of people stood in the rain and watched Snow White's coffin pass by.

The seven jazz-men, their hearts broken, carried the coffin unsteadily up the church steps. Suddenly one of them stumbled and dropped the coffin. The lid opened, and, to everyone's amazement, Snow White opened her eyes.

The first person she saw was the reporter.

He smiled at her and she smiled back.

The poisoned cherry that had been stuck in her throat was gone. She was alive.

Snow White and the reporter fell in love. They had a big wedding, and the next day cruised off on a glorious honeymoon together.

From *Snow White in New York* by Fiona French

Questions

Fill in the blanks

Snow White ______________ in New York. One day her father got ______________ again. Snow White's stepmother was very ______________ of her. She told one of her ______________ to ______________ Snow White. He took her into the dark streets and ______________ her there. Seven ______________ told Snow White she would be safe with them. When Snow White ______________ at the club a ______________ saw her. The stepmother saw a picture of Snow White in the New York ______________. She ______________ a party in ______________ of Snow White. She tried to ______________ Snow White by putting a ______________ cherry in her drink.

More Questions

1 The author says 'Snow White was a poor little rich girl.' What does this mean? How could she be both poor and rich?

2. Was the New York Mirror really a mirror? How can you tell?

3. Why was the stepmother jealous of Snow White?

Longer Writing

1. Did you like the story?

Remember!

When you answer a question 'Do you like..?' it is not enough to say just YES or NO.

You need to explain your reasons.

A good example:

I like ice cream because it is cold. In a hot summer it can cool me down.

2. What do you think happened to the Step Mother?

A Letters Page

Some newspapers have letters pages where readers can write their opinions. Read this information about Red Foxes and then read two letters sent to a newspaper.

The Red Fox is dog-like in appearance. It has pointed ears, a narrow muzzle and a bushy, white tipped tail.

The Red Fox measures about 120 cm in length and has a shoulder height of up to 40 cm. A fully grown fox weighs about 10 kg. Its color is usually reddish brown with a white chest and stomach.

The presence of a fox may be detected by its tracks, the scattered remains of food around its den, a distinctive musty smell, and long twisted droppings containing hair, bone and insect remains.

The Red Fox is found throughout Europe. It lives in a variety of habitats, usually in places where there is plenty of cover. In many places it ventures into villages and towns for food.

The fox is a carnivore (meat-eater), whose diet consists mainly of rodents but a variety of larger animals and fruit are eaten.

SIR, Foxes are a pest. They steal chickens from farms and raid dustbins in towns. The serve no useful purpose and should be destroyed. Yours Faithfully, Tim Brown	SIR, I believe that all life should be protected and that it is unnecessary to kill foxes. Leave foxes alone! Yours Faithfully, Sammy Smith

Words

Before we answer any questions let's see if you can guess the meaning of these difficult words. Look back at the words in the story and try to understand the meaning from the sentence.

muzzle ______________________________

bushy ______________________________

presence ______________________________

droppings ______________________________

habitats ______________________________

rodents ______________________________

Questions

FACTS ABOUT THE RED FOX	
Length	
Height	
Weight	
Special Features (Color etc.)	
Name of home	
Food eaten	
Usual habitat	

Some people think that red foxes should be killed. Others disagree. Choose two animals, and make a case for saving or killing them.

Have some fun!

We're going to do an activity– called choices. Your teacher is going to ask a question and you have to decide if you agree or disagree....and why!

A Newspaper

You are going to make a newspaper! Before you start let's learn some newspaper words:

Newspaper's Name Every newspaper needs to have a name! You can make a name yourself or copy a famous newspaper.

Date and Issue Number It is important for a newspaper to have a date - WHY? - and newspapers also have an issue number (you're newspaper will be issue number 1)

Headline A headline is extremely important. If the headline is boring no-one will read your story! You need to create a headline that is interesting and intriguing, but that does NOT give away the whole story. You could try alliteration, rhymes, jokes, idioms or more to create a catchy headline. Headlines are often written in ALL CAPS.

Byline The byline is the person who wrote the story. Not all stories have bylines, but the main stories in a newspaper usually do.

Picture Pictures can be helpful. They can help explain about the story, and they can also help catch the reader's eye. Make sure your picture is relevant

Caption Under the picture you must have a caption. This is a short sentence that explains the picture..

Now you should be ready to start writing your very own newspaper!

Turn to the next page to make your newspaper. You could write a story about Snow White, or about foxes, or anything else you like.

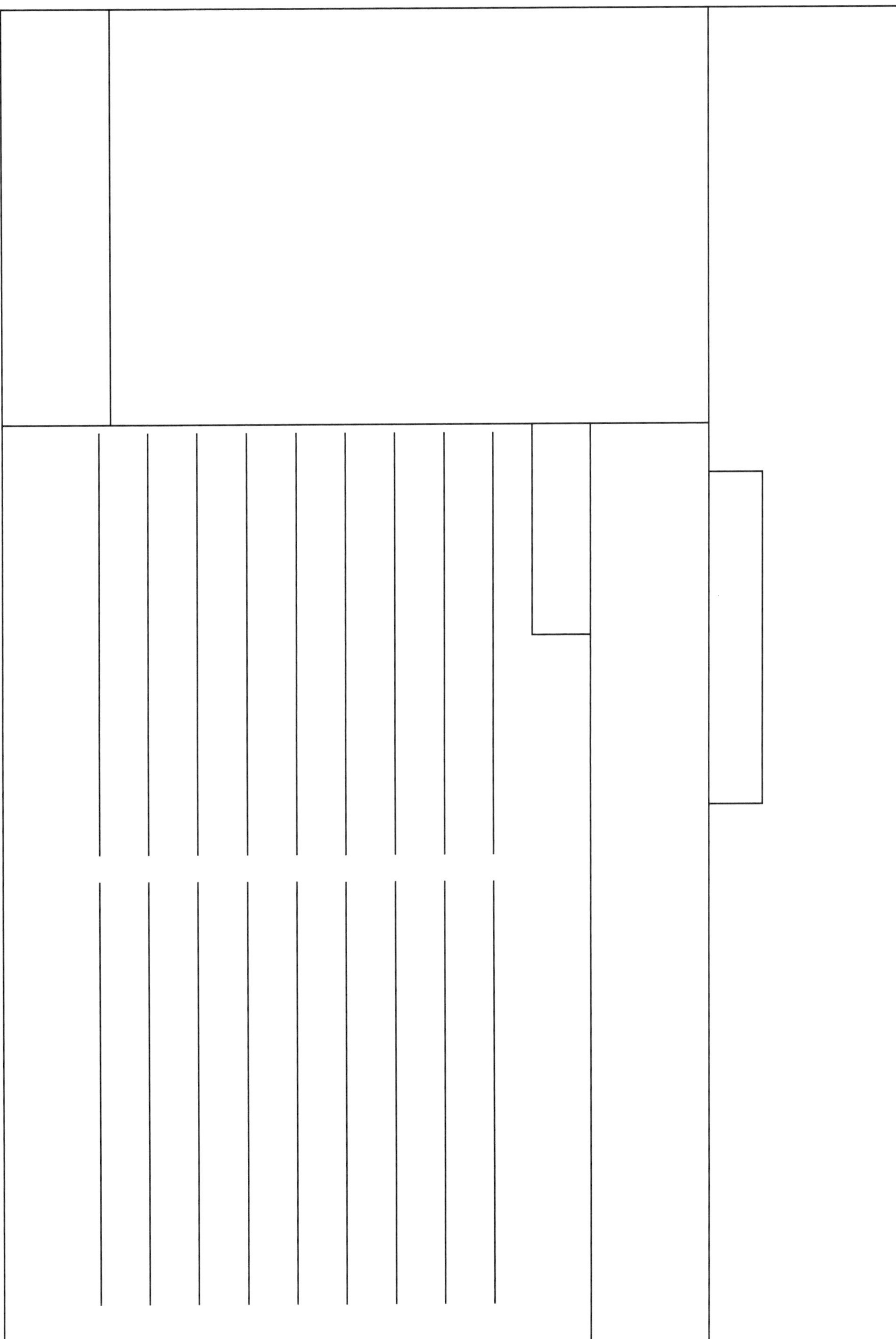

Don't lose them!

Put your mini flashcards here once you have cut them out

Mini Flashcards

talked to friends	done my homework
run	bought some shoes
eaten a bun	gone shopping
written my name	read a book

More writing

If you need any more space to write, then use these pages

Completion of
Mark's Mad Holiday
This certificate is presented to
For completing the 'Food' unit
BUS 10
SCHOOL
Crayons

http://ezbooks.me

ezBooks

Regal Court Business Centre

Tian He

Guangzhou

China

Mark's Mad Holidays Level 9 - Newspapers

First published March 2013

ISBN 978-1-300-68207-3

Project Manager: Mark Revis

Art Editor: Betty Long

Production Manager: Tara Chen

www.ingramcontent.com/pod-product-compliance
Ingram Content Group UK Ltd.
Pitfield, Milton Keynes, MK11 3LW, UK
UKHW060122300726
14090UKWH00002B/316

* 9 7 8 1 3 0 0 6 8 2 0 7 3 *